VIOLIN

101 POPULAR SONGS

Available for
FLUTE, CLARINET, ALTO SAX, TENOR SAX, TRUMPET,
HORN, TROMBONE, VIOLIN, VIOLA, CELLO

ISBN 978-1-4950-9030-1

7777 W. BLUEMOUND RD. P.O. BOX 13819 MILWAUKEE, WI 53213

Visit Hal Leonard Online at
www.halleonard.com

CONTENTS

ABC

VIOLIN

Words and Music by ALPHONSO MIZELL,
FREDERICK PERREN, DEKE RICHARDS
and BERRY GORDY

AFTERNOON DELIGHT

VIOLIN

Words and Music by
BILL DANOFF

AIN'T NO SUNSHINE

Violin

Words and Music by
BILL WITHERS

ALL YOU NEED IS LOVE

VIOLIN

Words and Music by JOHN LENNON
and PAUL McCARTNEY

AIN'T TOO PROUD TO BEG

VIOLIN

Words and Music by EDWARD HOLLAND JR.
and NORMAN WHITFIELD

ALL NIGHT LONG
(All Night)

VIOLIN

Words and Music by
LIONEL RICHIE

ANOTHER BRICK IN THE WALL

VIOLIN

Words and Music by
ROGER WATERS

Moderately

AT SEVENTEEN

VIOLIN

Words and Music by
JANIS IAN

BAD, BAD LEROY BROWN

VIOLIN

Words and Music by
JIM CROCE

BIG GIRLS DON'T CRY

VIOLIN

Words and Music by BOB CREWE
and BOB GAUDIO

BILLIE JEAN

VIOLIN

Words and Music by
MICHAEL JACKSON

BRIDGE OVER TROUBLED WATER

VIOLIN

Words and Music by
PAUL SIMON

CALIFORNIA DREAMIN'

Violin

Words and Music by JOHN PHILLIPS
and MICHELLE PHILLIPS

CARIBBEAN QUEEN
(No More Love on the Run)

VIOLIN

Words and Music by KEITH VINCENT ALEXANDER
and BILLY OCEAN

CENTERFOLD

Violin

Words and Music by
SETH JUSTMAN

COPACABANA
(At the Copa)

VIOLIN

Music by BARRY MANILOW
Lyric by BRUCE SUSSMAN and JACK FELDMAN

Moderately, with a Latin feel

CRACKLIN' ROSIE

Violin

Words and Music by
NEIL DIAMOND

DO YOU BELIEVE IN MAGIC

VIOLIN

Words and Music by
JOHN SEBASTIAN

DOWNTOWN

Violin

Words and Music by
TONY HATCH

DOWN UNDER

VIOLIN

Words and Music by COLIN HAY
and RON STRYKERT

DUST IN THE WIND

Words and Music by
KERRY LIVGREN

VIOLIN

THE FIRST TIME EVER I SAW YOUR FACE

VIOLIN

Words and Music by
EWAN MacCOLL

EASY

VIOLIN

Words and Music by
LIONEL RICHIE

FREE BIRD

Violin

Words and Music by ALLEN COLLINS
and RONNIE VAN ZANT

GENTLE ON MY MIND

VIOLIN

Words and Music by
JOHN HARTFORD

Moderately bright, in 2

GIRLS JUST WANT TO HAVE FUN

VIOLIN

Words and Music by
ROBERT HAZARD

GOD ONLY KNOWS

VIOLIN

Words and Music by BRIAN WILSON
and TONY ASHER

GROOVIN'

VIOLIN

Words and Music by FELIX CAVALIERE
and EDWARD BRIGATI, JR.

HAPPY TOGETHER

VIOLIN

Words and Music by GARRY BONNER
and ALAN GORDON

HEY JUDE

VIOLIN

Words and Music by JOHN LENNON
and PAUL McCARTNEY

I GET AROUND

VIOLIN

Words and Music by BRIAN WILSON
and MIKE LOVE

I HEARD IT THROUGH THE GRAPEVINE

VIOLIN

Words and Music by NORMAN J. WHITFIELD
and BARRETT STRONG

I SAW HER STANDING THERE

VIOLIN

Words and Music by JOHN LENNON
and PAUL McCARTNEY

I STILL HAVEN'T FOUND WHAT I'M LOOKING FOR

VIOLIN

Words and Music by
U2

I'M A BELIEVER

Violin

Words and Music by
NEIL DIAMOND

I WILL SURVIVE

VIOLIN

Words and Music by DINO FEKARIS
and FREDERICK J. PERREN

IF

VIOLIN

Words and Music by
DAVID GATES

Moderately, with feeling

IMAGINE

VIOLIN

Words and Music by
JOHN LENNON

Medium slow

JESSIE'S GIRL

VIOLIN

Words and Music by
RICK SPRINGFIELD

JUST ONCE

VIOLIN

Words by CYNTHIA WEIL
Music by BARRY MANN

KARMA CHAMELEON

VIOLIN

Words and Music by GEORGE O'DOWD,
JONATHAN MOSS, MICHAEL CRAIG,
ROY HAY and PHIL PICKETT

Moderately fast

KILLING ME SOFTLY WITH HIS SONG

VIOLIN

Words by NORMAN GIMBEL
Music by CHARLES FOX

LADY

VIOLIN

Words and Music by
LIONEL RICHIE

LAY DOWN SALLY

VIOLIN

Words and Music by ERIC CLAPTON,
MARCY LEVY and GEORGE TERRY

Moderately fast

LEADER OF THE PACK

VIOLIN

Words and Music by GEORGE MORTON,
JEFF BARRY and ELLIE GREENWICH

LEAN ON ME

Violin

Words and Music by
BILL WITHERS

LEAVING ON A JET PLANE

Violin

Words and Music by
JOHN DENVER

LET'S HANG ON

VIOLIN

Words and Music by BOB CREWE,
DENNY RANDELL and SANDY LINZER

LET'S HEAR IT FOR THE BOY
from the Paramount Motion Picture FOOTLOOSE

VIOLIN

Words by DEAN PITCHFORD
Music by TOM SNOW

Moderately fast

LIKE A VIRGIN

VIOLIN

Words and Music by BILLY STEINBERG
and TOM KELLY

THE LION SLEEPS TONIGHT

VIOLIN

New Lyrics and Revised Music by GEORGE DAVID WEISS,
HUGO PERETTI and LUIGI CREATORE

LIVIN' ON A PRAYER

VIOLIN

Words and Music by JON BON JOVI,
DESMOND CHILD and RICHIE SAMBORA

LOVE WILL KEEP US TOGETHER

Violin

Words and Music by NEIL SEDAKA
and HOWARD GREENFIELD

MANDY

VIOLIN

Words and Music by SCOTT ENGLISH
and RICHARD KERR

MANEATER

VIOLIN

Words and Music by SARA ALLEN,
DARYL HALL and JOHN OATES

MR. TAMBOURINE MAN

VIOLIN

Words and Music by
BOB DYLAN

MONDAY, MONDAY

VIOLIN

Words and Music by
JOHN PHILLIPS

MONY, MONY

VIOLIN

Words and Music by BOBBY BLOOM,
TOMMY JAMES, RITCHIE CORDELL
and BO GENTRY

MY CHERIE AMOUR

VIOLIN

Words and Music by STEVIE WONDER,
SYLVIA MOY and HENRY COSBY

MY GIRL

VIOLIN

Words and Music by SMOKEY ROBINSON
and RONALD WHITE

NIGHTS IN WHITE SATIN

Violin

Words and Music by
JUSTIN HAYWARD

Slowly, in 2

NIGHTSHIFT

VIOLIN

Words and Music by WALTER ORANGE,
FRANNE GOLDE and DENNIS LAMBERT

ONE MORE NIGHT

VIOLIN

Words and Music by
PHIL COLLINS

PHYSICAL

VIOLIN

Words and Music by STEPHEN A. KIPNER
and TERRY SHADDICK

PIANO MAN

VIOLIN

Words and Music by
BILLY JOEL

POUR SOME SUGAR ON ME

VIOLIN

Words and Music by JOE ELLIOTT,
PHIL COLLEN, RICHARD SAVAGE,
RICHARD ALLEN, STEVE CLARK
and R.J. LANGE

REELING IN THE YEARS

VIOLIN

Words and Music by WALTER BECKER
and DONALD FAGEN

RIGHT HERE WAITING

VIOLIN

Words and Music by
RICHARD MARX

Moderately

ROCKET MAN
(I Think It's Gonna Be a Long Long Time)

VIOLIN

Words and Music by ELTON JOHN
and BERNIE TAUPIN

SAVING ALL MY LOVE FOR YOU

Words by GERRY GOFFIN
Music by MICHAEL MASSER

Violin

Slowly, in 2

To Coda

D.S. al Coda
(no repeat)

CODA

SHE DRIVES ME CRAZY

VIOLIN

Words and Music by DAVID STEELE
and ROLAND GIFT

SHINY HAPPY PEOPLE

VIOLIN

Words and Music by WILLIAM BERRY,
PETER BUCK, MICHAEL MILLS
and MICHAEL STIPE

SILLY LOVE SONGS

VIOLIN

Words and Music by PAUL McCARTNEY
and LINDA McCARTNEY

D.C. al Coda

CODA

SISTER CHRISTIAN

VIOLIN

Words and Music by
KELLY KEAGY

Moderately slow

(Sittin' On)
THE DOCK OF THE BAY

VIOLIN

Words and Music by STEVE CROPPER
and OTIS REDDING

SMOKE ON THE WATER

VIOLIN

Words and Music by RITCHIE BLACKMORE,
IAN GILLAN, ROGER GLOVER,
JON LORD and IAN PAICE

SOMEBODY TO LOVE

Violin

Words and Music by
FREDDIE MERCURY

Moderately, in 2

SON-OF-A-PREACHER MAN

VIOLIN

Words and Music by JOHN HURLEY
and RONNIE WILKINS

THE SOUND OF SILENCE

VIOLIN

Words and Music by
PAUL SIMON

STAND BY ME

VIOLIN

Words and Music by JERRY LEIBER,
MIKE STOLLER and BEN E. KING

SWEET DREAMS
(Are Made of This)

VIOLIN

Words and Music by ANNIE LENNOX
and DAVID STEWART

SWEET HOME ALABAMA

Violin

Words and Music by RONNIE VAN ZANT,
ED KING and GARY ROSSINGTON

TAKE ME HOME, COUNTRY ROADS

Violin

Words and Music by JOHN DENVER,
BILL DANOFF and TAFFY NIVERT

Moderately, in 2

THESE DREAMS

VIOLIN

Words and Music by MARTIN GEORGE PAGE
and BERNIE TAUPIN

Moderately slow, in 2

THROUGH THE YEARS

VIOLIN

Words and Music by STEVE DORFF
and MARTY PANZER

TICKET TO RIDE

VIOLIN

Words and Music by JOHN LENNON
and PAUL McCARTNEY

TIME AFTER TIME

VIOLIN

Words and Music by CYNDI LAUPER
and ROB HYMAN

Moderately fast Rock

TIME IN A BOTTLE

Violin

Words and Music by
JIM CROCE

TRAVELIN' MAN

VIOLIN

Words and Music by
JERRY FULLER

25 OR 6 TO 4

VIOLIN

Words and Music by
ROBERT LAMM

UP, UP AND AWAY

VIOLIN

Words and Music by
JIMMY WEBB

WE'RE NOT GONNA TAKE IT

VIOLIN

Words and Music by
DANIEL DEE SNIDER

WHAT'S LOVE GOT TO DO WITH IT

VIOLIN

Words and Music by GRAHAM LYLE
and TERRY BRITTEN

A WHITER SHADE OF PALE

Violin

Words and Music by KEITH REID,
GARY BROOKER and MATTHEW FISHER

WICHITA LINEMAN

Violin

Words and Music by
JIMMY WEBB

Moderately slow

WITH OR WITHOUT YOU

VIOLIN

Words and Music by
U2

YESTERDAY

VIOLIN

Words and Music by JOHN LENNON
and PAUL McCARTNEY

Moderately, with expression

YOU ARE SO BEAUTIFUL

Violin

Words and Music by BILLY PRESTON
and BRUCE FISHER

YOU CAN'T HURRY LOVE

Violin

Words and Music by EDWARD HOLLAND JR.,
LAMONT DOZIER and BRIAN HOLLAND

YOU REALLY GOT ME

VIOLIN

Words and Music by
RAY DAVIES

YOU'RE SO VAIN

Violin

Words and Music by
CARLY SIMON

101 SONGS

BIG COLLECTIONS OF FAVORITE SONGS
ARRANGED FOR SOLO INSTRUMENTALISTS.

101 BROADWAY SONGS

00154199 Flute	$15.99
00154200 Clarinet	$15.99
00154201 Alto Sax	$15.99
00154202 Tenor Sax	$16.99
00154203 Trumpet	$15.99
00154204 Horn	$15.99
00154205 Trombone	$15.99
00154206 Violin	$15.99

00154207 Viola..................................$15.99
00154208 Cello..................................$15.99

101 DISNEY SONGS

00244104 Flute	$17.99
00244106 Clarinet	$17.99
00244107 Alto Sax	$17.99
00244108 Tenor Sax	$17.99
00244109 Trumpet	$17.99
00244112 Horn	$17.99
00244120 Trombone	$17.99
00244121 Violin	$17.99

00244125 Viola..................................$17.99
00244126 Cello..................................$17.99

101 MOVIE HITS

00158087 Flute	$15.99
00158088 Clarinet	$15.99
00158089 Alto Sax	$15.99
00158090 Tenor Sax	$15.99
00158091 Trumpet	$15.99
00158092 Horn	$15.99
00158093 Trombone	$15.99
00158094 Violin	$15.99

00158095 Viola..................................$15.99
00158096 Cello..................................$15.99

101 CHRISTMAS SONGS

00278637 Flute	$15.99
00278638 Clarinet	$15.99
00278639 Alto Sax	$15.99
00278640 Tenor Sax	$15.99
00278641 Trumpet	$15.99
00278642 Horn	$14.99
00278643 Trombone	$15.99
00278644 Violin	$15.99

00278645 Viola..................................$15.99
00278646 Cello..................................$15.99

101 HIT SONGS

00194561 Flute	$17.99
00197182 Clarinet	$17.99
00197183 Alto Sax	$17.99
00197184 Tenor Sax	$17.99
00197185 Trumpet	$17.99
00197186 Horn	$17.99
00197187 Trombone	$17.99
00197188 Violin	$17.99

00197189 Viola..................................$17.99
00197190 Cello..................................$17.99

101 POPULAR SONGS

00224722 Flute	$17.99
00224723 Clarinet	$17.99
00224724 Alto Sax	$17.99
00224725 Tenor Sax	$17.99
00224726 Trumpet	$17.99
00224727 Horn	$17.99
00224728 Trombone	$17.99
00224729 Violin	$17.99

00224730 Viola..................................$17.99
00224731 Cello..................................$17.99

101 CLASSICAL THEMES

00155315 Flute	$15.99
00155317 Clarinet	$15.99
00155318 Alto Sax	$15.99
00155319 Tenor Sax	$15.99
00155320 Trumpet	$15.99
00155321 Horn	$15.99
00155322 Trombone	$15.99
00155323 Violin	$15.99

00155324 Viola..................................$15.99
00155325 Cello..................................$15.99

101 JAZZ SONGS

00146363 Flute	$15.99
00146364 Clarinet	$15.99
00146366 Alto Sax	$15.99
00146367 Tenor Sax	$15.99
00146368 Trumpet	$15.99
00146369 Horn	$14.99
00146370 Trombone	$15.99
00146371 Violin	$15.99

00146372 Viola..................................$15.99
00146373 Cello..................................$15.99

101 MOST BEAUTIFUL SONGS

00291023 Flute	$16.99
00291041 Clarinet	$16.99
00291042 Alto Sax	$17.99
00291043 Tenor Sax	$17.99
00291044 Trumpet	$16.99
00291045 Horn	$16.99
00291046 Trombone	$16.99
00291047 Violin	$16.99

00291048 Viola..................................$16.99
00291049 Cello..................................$17.99

See complete song lists and sample pages at www.halleonard.com

HAL•LEONARD®
www.halleonard.com

HAL•LEONARD INSTRUMENTAL PLAY-ALONG

Your favorite songs are arranged just for solo instrumentalists with this outstanding series. Each book includes great full-accompaniment play-along audio so you can sound just like a pro!

Check out **halleonard.com** for songlists and more titles!

12 Pop Hits
12 songs
00261790	Flute	00261795	Horn
00261791	Clarinet	00261796	Trombone
00261792	Alto Sax	00261797	Violin
00261793	Tenor Sax	00261798	Viola
00261794	Trumpet	00261799	Cello

The Very Best of Bach
15 selections
00225371	Flute	00225376	Horn
00225372	Clarinet	00225377	Trombone
00225373	Alto Sax	00225378	Violin
00225374	Tenor Sax	00225379	Viola
00225375	Trumpet	00225380	Cello

The Beatles
15 songs
00225330	Flute	00225335	Horn
00225331	Clarinet	00225336	Trombone
00225332	Alto Sax	00225337	Violin
00225333	Tenor Sax	00225338	Viola
00225334	Trumpet	00225339	Cello

Chart Hits
12 songs
00146207	Flute	00146212	Horn
00146208	Clarinet	00146213	Trombone
00146209	Alto Sax	00146214	Violin
00146210	Tenor Sax	00146211	Trumpet
00146216	Cello		

Christmas Songs
12 songs
00146855	Flute	00146863	Horn
00146858	Clarinet	00146864	Trombone
00146859	Alto Sax	00146866	Violin
00146860	Tenor Sax	00146867	Viola
00146862	Trumpet	00146868	Cello

Contemporary Broadway
15 songs
00298704	Flute	00298709	Horn
00298705	Clarinet	00298710	Trombone
00298706	Alto Sax	00298711	Violin
00298707	Tenor Sax	00298712	Viola
00298708	Trumpet	00298713	Cello

Disney Movie Hits
12 songs
00841420	Flute	00841424	Horn
00841687	Oboe	00841425	Trombone
00841421	Clarinet	00841426	Violin
00841422	Alto Sax	00841427	Viola
00841686	Tenor Sax	00841428	Cello
00841423	Trumpet		

Prices, contents, and availability subject to change without notice.

Disney characters and artwork ™ & © 2021 Disney

Disney Solos
12 songs
00841404	Flute	00841506	Oboe
00841406	Alto Sax	00841409	Trumpet
00841407	Horn	00841410	Violin
00841411	Viola	00841412	Cello
00841405	Clarinet/Tenor Sax		
00841408	Trombone/Baritone		
00841553	Mallet Percussion		

Dixieland Favorites
15 songs
00268756	Flute	0068759	Trumpet
00268757	Clarinet	00268760	Trombone
00268758	Alto Sax		

Billie Eilish
9 songs
00345648	Flute	00345653	Horn
00345649	Clarinet	00345654	Trombone
00345650	Alto Sax	00345655	Violin
00345651	Tenor Sax	00345656	Viola
00345652	Trumpet	00345657	Cello

Favorite Movie Themes
13 songs
00841166	Flute	00841168	Trumpet
00841167	Clarinet	00841170	Trombone
00841169	Alto Sax	00841296	Violin

Gospel Hymns
15 songs
00194648	Flute	00194654	Trombone
00194649	Clarinet	00194655	Violin
00194650	Alto Sax	00194656	Viola
00194651	Tenor Sax	00194657	Cello
00194652	Trumpet		

Great Classical Themes
15 songs
00292727	Flute	00292733	Horn
00292728	Clarinet	00292735	Trombone
00292729	Alto Sax	00292736	Violin
00292730	Tenor Sax	00292737	Viola
00292732	Trumpet	00292738	Cello

The Greatest Showman
8 songs
00277389	Flute	00277394	Horn
00277390	Clarinet	00277395	Trombone
00277391	Alto Sax	00277396	Violin
00277392	Tenor Sax	00277397	Viola
00277393	Trumpet	00277398	Cello

Irish Favorites
31 songs
00842489	Flute	00842495	Trombone
00842490	Clarinet	00842496	Violin
00842491	Alto Sax	00842497	Viola
00842493	Trumpet	00842498	Cello
00842494	Horn		

Michael Jackson
11 songs
00119495	Flute	00119499	Trumpet
00119496	Clarinet	00119501	Trombone
00119497	Alto Sax	00119503	Violin
00119498	Tenor Sax	00119502	Accomp.

Jazz & Blues
14 songs
00841438	Flute	00841441	Trumpet
00841439	Clarinet	00841443	Trombone
00841440	Alto Sax	00841444	Violin
00841442	Tenor Sax		

Jazz Classics
12 songs
00151812	Flute	00151816	Trumpet
00151813	Clarinet	00151818	Trombone
00151814	Alto Sax	00151819	Violin
00151815	Tenor Sax	00151821	Cello

Les Misérables
13 songs
00842292	Flute	00842297	Horn
00842293	Clarinet	00842298	Trombone
00842294	Alto Sax	00842299	Violin
00842295	Tenor Sax	00842300	Viola
00842296	Trumpet	00842301	Cello

Metallica
12 songs
02501327	Flute	02502454	Horn
02501339	Clarinet	02501329	Trombone
02501332	Alto Sax	02501334	Violin
02501333	Tenor Sax	02501335	Viola
02501330	Trumpet	02501338	Cello

Motown Classics
15 songs
00842572	Flute	00842576	Trumpet
00842573	Clarinet	00842578	Trombone
00842574	Alto Sax	00842579	Violin
00842575	Tenor Sax		

Pirates of the Caribbean
16 songs
00842183	Flute	00842188	Horn
00842184	Clarinet	00842189	Trombone
00842185	Alto Sax	00842190	Violin
00842186	Tenor Sax	00842191	Viola
00842187	Trumpet	00842192	Cello

Queen
17 songs
00285402	Flute	00285407	Horn
00285403	Clarinet	00285408	Trombone
00285404	Alto Sax	00285409	Violin
00285405	Tenor Sax	00285410	Viola
00285406	Trumpet	00285411	Cello

Simple Songs
14 songs
00249081	Flute	00249087	Horn
00249093	Oboe	00249089	Trombone
00249082	Clarinet	00249090	Violin
00249083	Alto Sax	00249091	Viola
00249084	Tenor Sax	00249092	Cello
00249086	Trumpet	00249094	Mallets

Superhero Themes
14 songs
00363195	Flute	00363200	Horn
00363196	Clarinet	00363201	Trombone
00363197	Alto Sax	00363202	Violin
00363198	Tenor Sax	00363203	Viola
00363199	Trumpet	00363204	Cello

Star Wars
16 songs
00350900	Flute	00350907	Horn
00350913	Oboe	00350908	Trombone
00350903	Clarinet	00350909	Violin
00350904	Alto Sax	00350910	Viola
00350905	Tenor Sax	00350911	Cello
00350906	Trumpet	00350914	Mallet

Taylor Swift
15 songs
00842532	Flute	00842537	Horn
00842533	Clarinet	00842538	Trombone
00842534	Alto Sax	00842539	Violin
00842535	Tenor Sax	00842540	Viola
00842536	Trumpet	00842541	Cello

Video Game Music
13 songs
00283877	Flute	00283883	Horn
00283878	Clarinet	00283884	Trombone
00283879	Alto Sax	00283885	Violin
00283880	Tenor Sax	00283886	Viola
00283882	Trumpet	00283887	Cello

Wicked
13 songs
00842236	Flute	00842241	Horn
00842237	Clarinet	00842242	Trombone
00842238	Alto Sax	00842243	Violin
00842239	Tenor Sax	00842244	Viola
00842240	Trumpet	00842245	Cello

HAL•LEONARD®

101 TIPS FROM HAL LEONARD

STUFF ALL THE PROS KNOW AND USE

Ready to take your skills to the next level? These books present valuable how-to insight that musicians of all styles and levels can benefit from. The text, photos, music, diagrams and accompanying audio provide a terrific, easy-to-use resource for a variety of topics.

101 HAMMOND B-3 TIPS
by Brian Charette
Topics include: funky scales and modes; unconventional harmonies; creative chord voicings; cool drawbar settings; ear-grabbing special effects; professional gigging advice; practicing effectively; making good use of the pedals; and much more!
00128918 Book/Online Audio $14.99

101 HARMONICA TIPS
by Steve Cohen
Topics include: techniques, position playing, soloing, accompaniment, the blues, equipment, performance, maintenance, and much more!
00821040 Book/Online Audio $17.99

101 CELLO TIPS—2ND EDITION
by Angela Schmidt
Topics include: bowing techniques, non-classical playing, electric cellos, accessories, gig tips, practicing, recording and much more!
00149094 Book/Online Audio $14.99

101 FLUTE TIPS
by Elaine Schmidt
Topics include: selecting the right flute for you, finding the right teacher, warm-up exercises, practicing effectively, taking good care of your flute, gigging advice, staying and playing healthy, and much more.
00119883 Book/CD Pack...................................$14.99

101 SAXOPHONE TIPS
by Eric Morones
Topics include: techniques; maintenance; equipment; practicing; recording; performance; and much more!
00311082 Book/CD Pack...................................$19.99

101 TRUMPET TIPS
by Scott Barnard
Topics include: techniques, articulation, tone production, soloing, exercises, special effects, equipment, performance, maintenance and much more.
00312082 Book/CD Pack...................................$14.99

101 UPRIGHT BASS TIPS
by Andy McKee
Topics include: right- and left-hand technique, improvising and soloing, practicing, proper care of the instrument, ear training, performance, and much more.
00102009 Book/Online Audio $14.99

101 BASS TIPS
by Gary Willis
Topics include: techniques, improvising and soloing, equipment, practicing, ear training, performance, theory, and much more.
00695542 Book/Online Audio $19.99

101 DRUM TIPS—2ND EDITION
Topics include: grooves, practicing, warming up, tuning, gear, performance, and much more!
00151936 Book/Online Audio $14.99

101 FIVE-STRING BANJO TIPS
by Fred Sokolow
Topics include: techniques, ear training, performance, and much more!
00696647 Book/CD Pack...................................$14.99

101 GUITAR TIPS
by Adam St. James
Topics include: scales, music theory, truss rod adjustments, proper recording studio set-ups, and much more. The book also features snippets of advice from some of the most celebrated guitarists and producers in the music business.
00695737 Book/Online Audio $17.99

101 MANDOLIN TIPS
by Fred Sokolow
Topics include: playing tips, practicing tips, accessories, mandolin history and lore, practical music theory, and much more!
00119493 Book/Online Audio $14.99

101 RECORDING TIPS
by Adam St. James
This book contains recording tips, suggestions, and advice learned firsthand from legendary producers, engineers, and artists. These tricks of the trade will improve anyone's home or pro studio recordings.
00311035 Book/CD Pack...................................$14.95

101 UKULELE TIPS
by Fred Sokolow with Ronny Schiff
Topics include: techniques, improvising and soloing, equipment, practicing, ear training, performance, uke history and lore, and much more!
00696596 Book/Online Audio $15.99

101 VIOLIN TIPS
by Angela Schmidt
Topics include: bowing techniques, non-classical playing, electric violins, accessories, gig tips, practicing, recording, and much more!
00842672 Book/CD Pack...................................$14.99

Prices, contents and availability subject to change without notice.

HAL•LEONARD®

www.halleonard.com

THE ULTIMATE COLLECTION OF
FAKE BOOKS

The Real Book – Sixth Edition

Hal Leonard proudly presents the first legitimate and legal editions of these books ever produced. These bestselling titles are mandatory for anyone who plays jazz! Over 400 songs, including: All By Myself • Dream a Little Dream of Me • God Bless the Child • Like Someone in Love • When I Fall in Love • and more.

00240221	Volume 1, C Instruments	$45.00
00240224	Volume 1, B♭ Instruments	$45.00
00240225	Volume 1, E♭ Instruments	$45.00
00240226	Volume 1, BC Instruments	$45.00

Go to halleonard.com to view all *Real Books* available

The Beatles Fake Book

200 of the Beatles' hits: All You Need Is Love • Blackbird • Can't Buy Me Love • Day Tripper • Eleanor Rigby • The Fool on the Hill • Hey Jude • In My Life • Let It Be • Michelle • Norwegian Wood (This Bird Has Flown) • Penny Lane • Revolution • She Loves You • Twist and Shout • With a Little Help from My Friends • Yesterday • and many more!
00240069 C Instruments $39.99

The Best Fake Book Ever

More than 1,000 songs from all styles of music: All My Loving • At the Hop • Cabaret • Dust in the Wind • Fever • Hello, Dolly • Hey Jude • King of the Road • Longer • Misty • Route 66 • Sentimental Journey • Somebody • Song Sung Blue • Spinning Wheel • Unchained Melody • We Will Rock You • What a Wonderful World • Wooly Bully • Y.M.C.A. • and more.
00290239 C Instruments $49.99
00240084 E♭ Instruments..........$49.95

The Celtic Fake Book

Over 400 songs from Ireland, Scotland and Wales: Auld Lang Syne • Barbara Allen • Danny Boy • Finnegan's Wake • The Galway Piper • Irish Rover • Loch Lomond • Molly Malone • My Bonnie Lies Over the Ocean • My Wild Irish Rose • That's an Irish Lullaby • and more. Includes Gaelic lyrics where applicable and a pronunciation guide.
00240153 C Instruments $25.00

Classic Rock Fake Book

Over 250 of the best rock songs of all time: American Woman • Beast of Burden • Carry On Wayward Son • Dream On • Free Ride • Hurts So Good • I Shot the Sheriff • Layla • My Generation • Nights in White Satin • Owner of a Lonely Heart • Rhiannon • Roxanne • Summer of '69 • We Will Rock You • You Ain't Seen Nothin' Yet • and lots more!
00240108 C Instruments $35.00

Classical Fake Book

This unprecedented, amazingly comprehensive reference includes over 850 classical themes and melodies for all classical music lovers. Includes everything from Renaissance music to Vivaldi and Mozart to Mendelssohn. Lyrics in the original language are included when appropriate.
00240044 ....$39.99

The Disney Fake Book

Even more Disney favorites, including: The Bare Necessities • Can You Feel the Love Tonight • Circle of Life • How Do You Know? • Let It Go • Part of Your World • Reflection • Some Day My Prince Will Come • When I See an Elephant Fly • You'll Be in My Heart • and many more.
00175311 C Instruments $34.99
Disney characters & artwork TM & © 2021 Disney

The Folksong Fake Book

Over 1,000 folksongs: Bury Me Not on the Lone Prairie • Clementine • The Erie Canal • Go, Tell It on the Mountain • Home on the Range • Kumbaya • Michael Row the Boat Ashore • Shenandoah • Simple Gifts • Swing Low, Sweet Chariot • When Johnny Comes Marching Home • Yankee Doodle • and many more.
00240151 ....$34.99

The Hal Leonard Real Jazz Standards Fake Book

Over 250 standards in easy-to-read authentic hand-written jazz engravings: Ain't Misbehavin' • Blue Skies • Crazy He Calls Me • Desafinado (Off Key) • Fever • How High the Moon • It Don't Mean a Thing (If It Ain't Got That Swing) • Lazy River • Mood Indigo • Old Devil Moon • Route 66 • Satin Doll • Witchcraft • and more.
00240161 C Instruments $45.00

The Hymn Fake Book

Nearly 1,000 multi-denominational hymns perfect for church musicians or hobbyists: Amazing Grace • Christ the Lord Is Risen Today • For the Beauty of the Earth • It Is Well with My Soul • A Mighty Fortress Is Our God • O for a Thousand Tongues to Sing • Praise to the Lord, the Almighty • Take My Life and Let It Be • What a Friend We Have in Jesus • and hundreds more!
00240145 C Instruments $29.99

The New Broadway Fake Book

This amazing collection includes 645 songs from 285 shows: All I Ask of You • Any Dream Will Do • Close Every Door • Consider Yourself • Dancing Queen • Mack the Knife • Mamma Mia • Memory • The Phantom of the Opera • Popular • Strike up the Band • and more!
00138905 C Instruments $45.00

The Praise & Worship Fake Book

Over 400 songs including: Amazing Grace (My Chains Are Gone) • Cornerstone • Everlasting God • Great Are You Lord • In Christ Alone • Mighty to Save • Open the Eyes of My Heart • Shine, Jesus, Shine • This Is Amazing Grace • and more.
00160838 C Instruments $39.99
00240324 B♭ Instruments..........$34.99

Three Chord Songs Fake Book

200 classic and contemporary 3-chord tunes in melody/lyric/chord format: Ain't No Sunshine • Bang a Gong (Get It On) • Cold, Cold Heart • Don't Worry, Be Happy • Give Me One Reason • I Got You (I Feel Good) • Kiss • Me and Bobby McGee • Rock This Town • Werewolves of London • You Don't Mess Around with Jim • and more.
00240387 ....$34.99

The Ultimate Christmas Fake Book

The 6th edition of this bestseller features over 270 traditional and contemporary Christmas hits: Have Yourself a Merry Little Christmas • I'll Be Home for Christmas O Come, All Ye Faithful (Adeste Fideles) • Santa Baby • Winter Wonderland • and more.
00147215 C Instruments $30.00

The Ultimate Country Fake Book

This book includes over 700 of your favorite country hits: Always on My Mind • Boot Scootin' Boogie • Crazy • Down at the Twist and Shout • Forever and Ever, Amen • Friends in Low Places • The Gambler • Jambalaya • King of the Road • Sixteen Tons • There's a Tear in My Beer • Your Cheatin' Heart • and hundreds more.
00240049 C Instruments $49.99

The Ultimate Fake Book

Includes over 1,200 hits: Blue Skies • Body and Soul • Endless Love • Isn't It Romantic? • Memory • Mona Lisa • Moon River • Operator • Piano Man • Roxanne • Satin Doll • Shout • Small World • Smile • Speak Softly, Love • Strawberry Fields Forever • Tears in Heaven • Unforgettable • hundreds more!
00240024 C Instruments $55.00
00240026 B♭ Instruments..........$49.95

The Ultimate Jazz Fake Book

This must-own collection includes 635 songs spanning all jazz styles from more than 9 decades. Songs include: Maple Leaf Rag • Basin Street Blues • A Night in Tunisia • Lullaby of Birdland • The Girl from Ipanema • Bag's Groove • I Can't Get Started • All the Things You Are • and many more!
00240079 C Instruments $45.00
00240080 B♭ Instruments $45.00
00240081 E♭ Instruments $45.00

The Ultimate Rock Pop Fake Book

This amazing collection features nearly 550 rock and pop hits: American Pie • Bohemian Rhapsody • Born to Be Wild • Clocks • Dancing with Myself • Eye of the Tiger • Proud Mary • Rocket Man • Should I Stay or Should I Go • Total Eclipse of the Heart • Unchained Melody • When Doves Cry • Y.M.C.A. • You Raise Me Up • and more.
00240310 C Instruments $39.99

**Complete songlists available online at
www.halleonard.com**